SHOW ME HOW

Mary Ruth's How to Knit Book

COMPLETE DiRECTioNS foR LeaRNiNG to KNit

Susan Levin and Gloria Tracy

sixth&spring books

We dedicate our *Show Me How* books to our mothers, Ruth Straumer Wagner and Mary Bridges Jensma. They inspired us to find a lifetime of pleasure, creative outlets and contentment in a wide range of crafts. We think they would be pleased to see another generation of budding crafters being inspired to carry on the tradition.

— SL and GT

Editorial Director: Elaine Silverstein

Copy Editor: Kristina Sigler

Book Division Manager: Erica Smith

Art Director, Project Manager: Nancy Sabato

Associate Editor: Amanda Keiser

Story Illustrations: Cathi Mingus

Technical Illustrations: John Rice

Vice President, Publisher: Trisha Malcolm

Creative Director: Joe Vior

Production Manager: David Joinnides

President, Sixth&Spring Books: Art Joinnides

Library of Congress Control Number: 2007921002

ISBN: 1-933027-27-4

ISBN-13: 978-1-933027-27-2

Manufactured in China

1 3 5 7 9 10 8 6 4 2

First Edition

Contents

Knitting for You and Me

Knitting is really easy once you get going.
I was lucky that my grandma helped me at first. If you know a grown-up or have a friend who can help you, that's great, but you can do it by yourself too. Just read the directions carefully!

There are lots of extra things that help make knitting easier and more fun when you make projects, but all you really need to get started are:

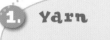

1. Yarn
2. Knitting Needles

It is easiest to start knitting with smooth yarn in a medium weight (it is sometimes called worsted weight or #4). Use size 7 or 8 needles. I'll explain what that means soon.

✱ Hey Lefties! ✱

It doesn't make any difference if you are left-handed when you knit, because you use both hands pretty much equally. My friend Keisha is left-handed and she learned with no trouble at all!

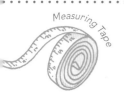

Measuring Tape

Scissors

Yarn needles

Ball

Log

Twist or Hank

When you buy yarn, it usually looks like one of these pictures on the right. They are all called **skeins**, but sometimes people call them other names too.

Sometimes balls and logs can be pulled from the center.

When you pull from the center, the skein stays in one place, so the yarn gets tangled less and is easier to work with.

Skein rhymes with rain.

If you buy yarn in a hank, you will need to wind it into a ball yourself.

Buying Yarn

Going to a store to buy yarn can be really confusing.

There are soooo many colors and kinds of yarn. If there is a salesperson around, she will help you, but you can learn to read a yarn label by yourself. Yarn labels have symbols that contain a lot of useful information.

Every ball of yarn has a label. The label will tell you what size of needles work best with the yarn and what the **gauge** is. Gauge means how many stitches and rows it takes to make 4 inches of knitting.

Manufacturer's Name

BRAND NAME

Fiber Content

Yarn Weight (ounces/grams)
Yarn Length (yards/meters)

Gauge and Needle Size

Care Instructions

Manufacturer's Address

Color Name/Number
Dyelot Number

Yarn label

Gauge rhymes with page.

This "4" symbol tells you the size, or weight, of the yarn.

The smaller the number, the thinner the yarn and the more stitches it will take to knit something.

The "4" symbol is for a medium-weight yarn. This weight is a good choice for learning to knit. I used it for my first project.

This symbol gives you two types of information. First, the "8 US" suggests what size of knitting needles to use. Size 8 needles are medium-sized, like the yarn they're used for. It is usually OK to use one size smaller or one size larger than what this label tells you, depending on the look and feel you want.

The "16 S" and "24 R" tells you how many stitches and how many rows you can expect to knit in 4 inches if you use the recommended needle size. That's the gauge. For this yarn, you could expect to get about 16 stitches in 4 inches. If you divide 16 by 4, you get 4 stitches per inch.

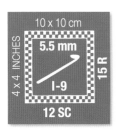

This symbol gives the same information for crochet. (That's fun to do too!)

*Look in **OS2K** (Other Stuff to Know) to learn how to figure out your personal gauge and to see a Yarn and Needle Chart.*

Getting Started

slipknot

Okay, you're almost ready to start knitting.

The first thing you have to do is cast on. That means getting some loops on the needles for the first row of stitches. You start by making a **slipknot**.

1

Make a loop in your yarn about 12" from the end by putting the yarn from the ball over the tail end.

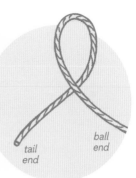

tail end

ball end

2 Fold the loop over so it crosses the short tail end.

3 Poke the tip of your needle under the tail.

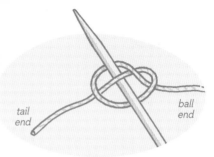

4 Pull on the tail end until the knot is snug against the bottom of the needle. Don't pull it too tight or it will be hard to knit into it.

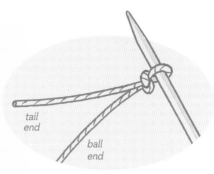

casting On

Once that first stitch is on your needle, it's time to cast on the rest of the row. There are lots of different ways to cast on. I think the easiest is the **E-wrap cast on**. It's called E-wrap because the loops look like "e"s. Here's how you do it:

1

Hold the needle with the slipknot in your right hand. Wrap the yarn from the ball around your thumb from front to back and hold it in your palm with your fingers.

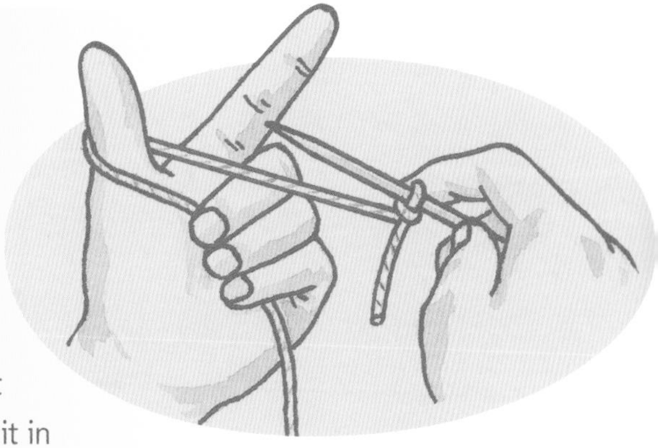

2 Push the needle upward through the yarn on your thumb. Now, slip the loop from your thumb onto the needle.

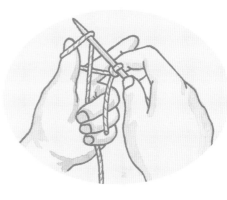

3 Pull the yarn from the ball to tighten it, but don't make it too tight or it will be hard to knit the first row. Keep doing this until all the loops you want are cast on.

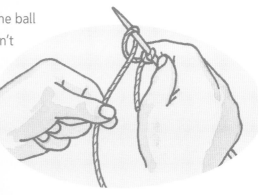

For now, cast on 12 stitches (loops) including the slipknot.
That's how many my brother Jacob and I used for our first projects.

Holding the Yarn and Needles

When you are ready to knit, hold the needle with the stitches in your left hand and the empty needle in your right hand.

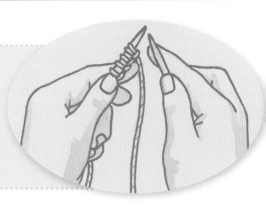

When you are wrapping the yarn around the needle, you pinch both needles together in your left hand so your right hand is free to wrap the yarn around the needle.

There are lots of different ways to hold the yarn as you wrap it around the needle.

The only rule is that there are no rules!

If what you're doing works for you, it's okay. I like that!

At first I just let the yarn fall loose between each stitch. You may want to do that too. Later, I learned a new way of holding the yarn. It felt really awkward at first, but once I got used to it, it made my stitches more even and helped me knit faster. I wrote directions for Another Way to Hold the Yarn in OS2K on page 38. Check it out.

Ready, set, KNIT!

I was surprised when I found out there are only two stitches that make up knitted projects — the **knit stitch** and the **purl stitch**!

KNIT likes the yarn in back!

I learned how to do the **KNIT stitch** with a rhyme that helped me remember what to do:

Poke tip to the back. ⇒ Loop yarn around the needle

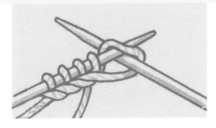
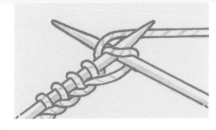

Keep saying the rhyme to yourself as you work each stitch from the left needle to the right until you get to the end of the row. **TA DA!** You did it! Good job!

Now switch the needle with all the stitches back to your left hand and start over. Knit about 10 rows. Your knitting will have rows of ridges, and it will look the same on both sides. Look at the picture on page 20 to see what it will look like.

The fronts of **KNIT stitches** *are flat and look like little hearts.*

(The backs of knit stitches are bumpy.)

Pull stitch out the front. ⇨ Push KNIT off full speedle!

The PURL stitch

Now you're ready for the **PURL stitch**. Purl stitches are the opposite of knit stitches — sort of.

PURL likes the yarn in front!

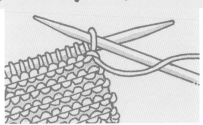

Use this rhyme to make **PURL stitches**:

All the sweaters, scarves, hats, afghans, socks and mittens you see are made from just putting these tw stitches together in different ways!

poke tip to the front.   Loop yarn over needle.

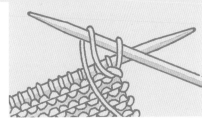

Keep doing that with each stitch until you get to the end of the row. **TA DA!** Now you know the basics!

Often, rows of purl stitches are alternated with rows of knit stitches. When you do this, your knitting looks flat on one side and bumpy on the other side. Look at the picture of this on the next page.

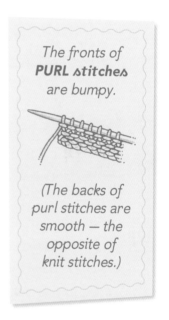

The fronts of **PURL stitches** *are bumpy.*

(The backs of purl stitches are smooth — the opposite of knit stitches.)

sweep stitch to the back. push purl off skadeedle!

what's Next?

Now you know how to **knit** and **purl**. That's just about all you need to know to make your first project. Keep practicing until you are comfortable making rows of knit stitches and rows of purl stitches.

Interesting things happen when you combine knit and purl. If you knit every row, your knitting will have bumpy ridges on both sides. This is called **garter stitch**.

The front and back of garter stitch look the same. Your knitting will lie flat.

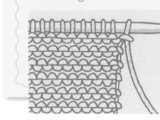

The front and back of stockinette stitch look different and the edges will curl.

If you knit one row and purl the next row, your knitting will be smooth on one side and bumpy on the other side. This is called **stockinette stitch**.

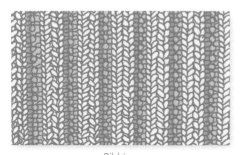
Ribbing

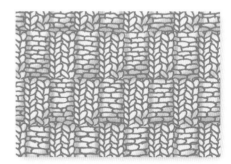
Basketweave Stitch

If you mix up knitting and purling you will start to make all different designs. You can also cross stitches over each other or make "holey" patterns. There are hundreds of different ways to make stitches!

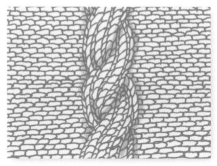
Cable

Lace

Look at some knitting books at your library or bookstore to see all the different patterns you can make.

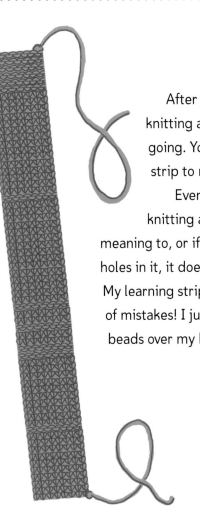

After you get pretty good at knitting and purling, just keep going. You can use your learning strip to make your first project. Even if you mixed up knitting and purling without meaning to, or if you have some holes in it, it doesn't matter. My learning strip sure had plenty of mistakes! I just sewed some beads over my holes. ☺

If you HATE your learning strip, pull out all the stitches and start fresh. It's not a big deal. Everyone's first project looks kind of funky.

My grandma showed me how to make my learning strip into a headband. To make a headband, knit until your strip is about one inch smaller than the distance around your head.

(Try it on as you knit to make it fit perfectly.)

My brother Jacob made his learning strip into an eyeglass case for our dad. To make an eyeglass case, knit until your strip is 12 inches long.

You can make presents for your friends and family!

Binding Off

When your strip is the length you want, you need to get it off the needles and end it so it doesn't fall apart. This is called **binding off**. There are lots of ways to bind off, but my grandma thinks this is the easiest one to learn.

1
Knit two stitches.
* Use your left needle to pick up the first stitch on the right needle.

2
Pull the first stitch over the second stitch and let it fall off the end of the left needle.

3
One stitch has been bound off, and you have one stitch on the right needle.

4

Knit one more stitch.
Now go back to the ✳
in Step 1.

5

Keep doing this until you
only have one stitch left
on the right needle. Make
sure you keep your stitches
really loose so your finished
piece won't be puckered.

6

Cut the yarn about 12 inches
away from your knitting.
Use your needle to pull the tail
through the last stitch and tighten.

Finishing

Okay! You're almost done.

To finish your headband or eyeglass case, you need to sew it together with a yarn needle. Decide which side of your strip you want on the outside and call it the right side. Fold the strip with the right side on the inside.

For a headband fold it this way.

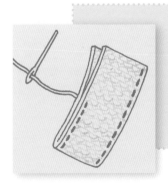

For a glasses case, fold it this way.

Your learning strip may look different from mine, depending on what combinations of knit and purl stitches you used to make it.

You can sew seams a couple of different ways (you will need a yarn needle). You decide which one you like best. One method of sewing is called **straight stitch**.

1

Thread an 18" piece of yarn on a yarn needle (or use the tail left over from binding off). To attach the new yarn, poke the needle from bottom to top, leaving a 3" tail on the bottom. Tie a knot.

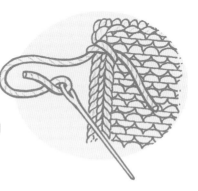

2

To sew seams using a straight stitch (also called running stitch), push the needle from top to bottom through both layers of knitting and pull it all the way through. Then push the needle up through the bottom and pull it back up. Make your stitches about a stitch or row apart. Keep doing this until you get to the end of the strip.

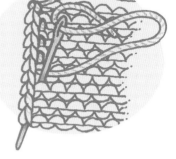

Another method of sewing is called **overcast** (also called **whip stitch**).

1 Start the same way as for straight stitch. Then take the needle over and around the edge to the back. Push it back up and pull it all the way through. Keep doing this until you get to the end.

2 For either kind of seam, leave a loop when you finish the last stitch. Put the needle through the loop and pull up tight to fasten off.

3 The last thing you have to do is weave in the ends of yarn left over from casting on and binding off. Do that for about 2 inches on the inside of your piece, then trim the ends.

TA DA! Now you've got a finished project and you know just about everything you need to know to make lots of things!

Other Projects to make

I wrote down the directions for four more projects you can make — the Barkley Ball, Kitty (or baby) Comforter, Hotsy-Totsy Hat and a longgggg Skinny Scarf.

When you read the directions, you'll see that I wrote them in a kind of shorthand. My grandma said I should do it that way because that's how knitting instructions are written in books and magazines. It saves lots of space and it sure was fast and easy once I got the hang of it! It reminds me of the way we write text messages. I'm sure you'll figure it out very fast. If you aren't sure what something means, there is a list of all the abbreviations in OS2K on page 46.

Barkley Ball

Jacob made this ball for his dog, Barkley, but it would also make a really cool gift for a baby.

Materials Needed

* #4 weight (worsted) yarn (approximately 3 ounces)
* Size 8 needles
* Yarn needle
* Stuffing (you can buy bags of polyester stuffing in craft stores)

Directions

• CO 20 sts leaving a 12" tail.

• K until piece is two times as long as it is wide.

• End your knitting on the opposite side from where the CO tail is. BO leaving 12" tail. Now you have two tails on the same side of your piece.

Finishing

• Fold in half with RS together. Sew the bound off edge and the cast on edge together with one of the tails. DON'T cut the yarn yet!

- Make a running stitch along one edge and pull to gather up. Fasten off and weave in the tail like it says on page 28.

- Turn the ball so the right side is out. Stuff the ball with purchased stuffing or cut-up nylon stockings. Close up the second side with the other tail by gathering up and sewing like you did on the first side.

There are lots of other neat things you can make with the same basic pattern.

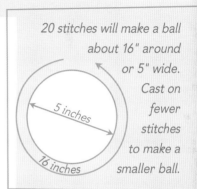

20 stitches will make a ball about 16" around or 5" wide. Cast on fewer stitches to make a smaller ball.

5 inches

16 inches

❋ Make a ball for a baby by putting a bell or marble inside an empty film canister or pill container. Wrap stuffing around the container and put it in the center of the ball.

❋ Cats would LOVE this ball with some catnip hidden in the middle. Pet stores sell catnip.

❋ Instead of a ball, you can make a bean bag. Sew the sides together flat. Put dried beans inside.

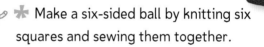

❋ Make a six-sided ball by knitting six squares and sewing them together.

Hotsy-Totsy Hat

Making this hat is easy, but it takes LOTS of stitches since it has to fit around your head. If you use straight needles, they will be very crowded, so be careful not to drop any stitches.

Circular Needle

This might be a good time to try a **circular needle**. Maybe you could borrow one from a friend or your grandma. A needle that is 18" or 24" long would work well.

Gauge is really important for this project. To make sure that your hat fits, check to see that your gauge is close to what is suggested on the ball band of your yarn. You can learn all about gauge in OS2K on page 43.

Materials Needed

* #4 weight (worsted) yarn (approximately 3 ounces)
* Size 8 needles (either straight or circular)
* Yarn needle

> *Just because you use a circular needle, it doesn't mean you have to knit around. You can knit back and forth with it too!*

Directions

- CO 80 sts.

- Knit in garter stitch for 1½".

- Change to stockinette stitch and knit for 6 more inches. Leave all your stitches on the needle and cut the yarn, leaving a 20" tail.

- Now be really careful with this next part. Thread the tail onto the yarn needle and very carefully transfer each of the stitches from 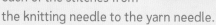 the knitting needle to the yarn needle.

- Now you can easily gather all those stitches up by pulling them all together. Decide which side is the RS, and hold the hat with the WS facing you. Fasten off the gathered stitches tightly on the wrong side, but DON'T cut the yarn yet. Use it to sew up the seam.

- Then fasten off and weave in the ends. Look on page 28 if you aren't sure how to do this.

- If you want, you can make a pompom for your hat. You can learn how to do that on page 40.

✱ Try This! ✱

*For fun, make
your pompom in
a different color.
Maybe you can trade yarn
colors with a friend.*

Tasseled skinny scarf

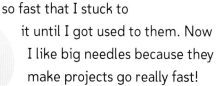

This scarf was the first time I used fluffy yarn (the one I used was called "eyelash"). I held together a strand of eyelash yarn and a strand of plain yarn in colors that looked pretty together to make the scarf. That made a really thick yarn, so I had to use big needles — size15! The big needles felt awkward at first, but the knitting went so fast that I stuck to it until I got used to them. Now I like big needles because they make projects go really fast!

Eyelash Yarn

Plain Yarn

Materials Needed

* Eyelash or other fluffy yarn, about 100 yards
* Plain #4 weight (worsted) yarn, about 100 yards
* Size 15 needles
* Yarn needle
* Crochet hook (for making fringe, if desired)

Crochet Hook

Directions

- Before you start knitting, cut off 10 yards of both yarns and put them aside. You'll use that yarn to make two tassels or fringe when you are done.

- Hold your fluffy yarn together with the plain yarn and CO 8 sts.

- If you knit every row (garter stitch) your scarf will lie flat and be about 2" wide. If you knit in stockinette stitch (knit one row, purl one row), your scarf will curl and look like a tube that is about 1" wide. You choose!

- Knit until your scarf is about 60" long OR the length you want it to be OR until you only have about 12" of yarn left. BO. Weave in ends.

Finishing

- Make fringe on each end (see page 41) or make two tassels (see page 42) and attach one to each end.

Kitty Comforter

I made this comforter for my cat, Phoebe, but you could also use these directions to make a comforter for your doll. Finished size is about 15" x 20". If you made it wider and longer, it could be for a new baby.

You can use three different colors of yarn or just one color. You can also use different stitches if you want to.

Materials Needed

* #4 weight (worsted) yarn — about 6 ounces total in the color or colors of your choice
* Size 8 needles
* Yarn needle
* Crochet hook (for making fringe, if desired)

Directions

* CO 20 sts. K for 20". BO.

* Repeat for 2 more strips. (That will make a total of 3 strips that are each 5" wide.)

* Sew the strips together. Weave in ends. Finish by making multicolored fringe on each end. The directions for fringe are on page 41.

OS2K
Other Stuff to Know

Another Way to Hold the Yarn

1 Wind the yarn around your right pinkie from front to back.

2 Next, wrap it behind and around your index finger.

3 Without letting the yarn unwind, pick up your needles and hold one in each hand.

4

After you poke the right needle into the first stitch on the left needle, use your right index finger to take the yarn around the needle without letting it come off your pinkie finger.

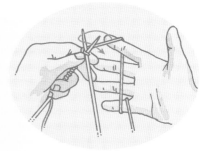

5

Finish by pulling the loop forward and then sliding the old stitch off the end of the left needle. The important thing about this way of holding the yarn is KEEP IT LOOSE. If the yarn gets too tight, your knitting will be too tight.

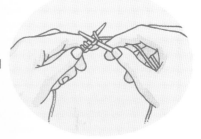

✳ Here's a tip! ✳

Remember, this method worked great for me, but you can do it however you like. Look at other people who knit to see how they do it. You'll be surprised at how many different ways you can hold your yarn!

Pompoms

Pompoms are easy to make in all different sizes. You can buy a pompom maker, or you can make your own like my grandma showed me.

1 Make two circles of cardboard the size you want your pompom to be. Cut out angled notches in both circles and an inside circle about an inch in diameter as shown.

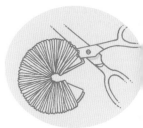

2 Hold the two circles together and wrap the yarn around them until the center hole is almost filled. Stick one blade of your scissors between the two pieces of cardboard and carefully cut around the outside. DON'T TAKE THE CARDBOARD OUT YET!

3 Slide a piece of yarn between the two pieces of cardboard and tie it in a tight knot around the yarn ball. NOW take the cardboard out and trim the pompom.

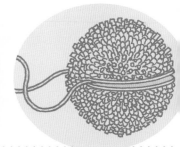

Fringe

Fringe is really easy and uses up lots of leftover yarn. All you need is a crochet hook and scissors.

1 Cut pieces of yarn slightly longer than twice the length you want your finished fringe to be. (For example, for 3" fringe, cut strips 7" long.) Gather two or three strands together and fold them in half.

2 Insert a crochet hook from back to front in the edge of your knitted piece. Catch the folded yarn in the hook and pull a loop through.

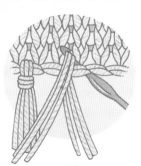

3 Use the crochet hook to pull the loose ends of yarn through the loop. Pull tight to form a knot. Repeat this along the edge of the piece. When you are finished, lay the piece flat and carefully trim the ends to neaten them.

Tassels

You can make big or little tassels just by changing the size of your cardboard and the amount of yarn you use.

1 Cut a piece of cardboard about 3" wide and the length you want your tassels to be. (5" is a pretty good length.) Cut a piece of yarn about 5 yards long and wrap it around the cardboard.

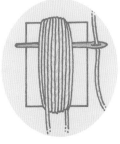

2 Thread a piece of yarn in a yarn needle. Slide it under the wrapped yarn and tie it at the top, leaving long tails to use to attach the tassel to your knitting. Cut the lower edge to free the wrapped strands.

3 About 1" below the top, wrap a piece of yarn tightly around the tassel two or three times and make a knot. Thread the tails into a yarn needle and push them to the inside of the tassel. Trim the ends.

Gauge

Gauge is the number of stitches and rows it takes to make one square inch of knitting. Sometimes it is also called tension. Lots of patterns and ball bands give the gauge for 4 inches of knitting. For instance, they might say it this way:

16 stitches and 24 rows = 4 inches.

The gauge on the ball band is just a suggestion. It's the gauge the yarn company thinks most people will get, using that yarn and that needle size. The gauge you actually get may be different.

Your gauge depends mainly on four things:

1. The size of needles you use
2. The thickness of yarn you use
3. How tight or loose you knit
4. The stitch pattern you choose

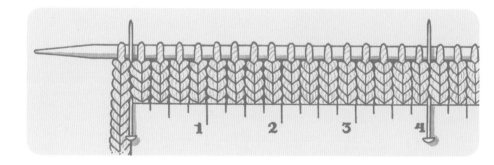

To figure out your gauge, cast on 24 stitches and knit a piece 6 inches long with the yarn, needles and stitch pattern you plan to use. Lay your knitting flat and smooth it out without stretching. Lay a ruler over your knitting and measure 4 inches by putting a straight pin or toothpick at the zero and 4 inch marks. Now count the number of stitches between your marks. The sample above shows 16 stitches between the markers.

Divide the number of stitches you counted by 4. That's your stitch gauge per inch.

If your gauge doesn't match what's recommended on the ball band or your pattern, look at the list of things that can affect your gauge and see if you can change something.

For instance, if you count 16 stitches in 4 inches, your gauge per inch would be 4 stitches (16 divided by 4). This means that with those needles and that yarn, it takes 4 stitches to make 1 inch.

If you want to make a piece 15" wide you would multiply 15 x 4. That makes 60. So you need to cast on 60 stitches.

Use the same process to figure out your row gauge.

There are two other things that may affect your gauge:

* How you hold your yarn
* How you are feeling

Relax and have fun!

If you are mad at somebody or nervous about school, your knitting might get really really tight!

Abbreviations

approx approximately

alt alternate

beg begin, beginning

BO bind off

cm centimeter

CO cast on

cont continue, continuing

dec decrease, decreases, decreasing

garter stitch (knit every row)

inc increase, increases, increasing

k knit

LH left hand

ndl needle, needles

oz ounce, ounces

p purl

pat pattern

rep repeat

RH right hand

RS right side

st, sts stitch, stitches

St st stockinette stitch (knit one row, purl one row)

tog together

WS wrong side

yd, yds yard, yards

" inch, inches

* repeat directions following * as many times as indicated

Standard Yarn Weight System

Categories of yarn, gauge ranges, and recommended needle and hook sizes

Yarn Weight Symbol & Category Names	**1** **Super Fine**	**2** **Fine**	**3** **Light**	**4** **Medium**	**5** **Bulky**	**6** **Super Bulky**
Type of Yarns in Category	Sock, Fingering, Baby	Sport, Baby	DK, Light Worsted	Worsted, Afghan, Aran	Chunky, Craft, Rug	Bulky, Roving
Knit Gauge Range* in Stockinette Stitch to 4 Inches	27–32 sts	23–26 sts	21–24 sts	16–20 sts	12–15 sts	6–11 sts
Recommended Needle in Metric Size Range	2.25–3.25 mm	3.25–3.75 mm	3.75–4.5 mm	4.5–5.5 mm	5.5–8 mm	8 mm and larger
Recommended Needle U.S. Size Range	1 to 3	3 to 5	5 to 7	7 to 9	9 to 11	11 and larger
Crochet Gauge* Ranges in Single Crochet To 4 Inch	21–32 sts	16–20 sts	12–17 sts	11–14 sts	8–11 sts	5–9 sts
Recommended Hook in Metric Size Range	2.25–3.5 mm	3.5–4.5 mm	4.5–5.5 mm	5.5–6.5 mm	6.5–9 mm	9 mm and larger
Recommended Hook U.S. Size Range	B–1 to E–4	E–4 to 7	7 to I–9	I–9 to K–10½	K–10½ to M–13	M–13 and larger

*GUIDELINES ONLY: The above reflect the most commonly used gauges and
 needle or hook sizes for specific yarn categories.

write to Mary Ruth!

Dear Knitting Friends,

If you've made a couple of projects in this book, you are ready to make anything you want! I'd love to see what you make. Send me a picture, describe your project, and tell me about the person who helped you learn to knit. You can also learn more about knitting, download fun patterns and find out about cool magazines, websites and charity organizations at www.showmehowcrafts.com.

HAPPY KNITTING!

XXOO

Mary Ruth

MaryRuth@showmehowcrafts.com